The Healthy Meal Prep Cookbook

The Healthy Meal Prep Cookbook

Make it Easy! Delicious and Simple Meals to Prep for Beginners.

Tanaya Hill

Copyright@2018 by Published in the United States by TANAYA HILL.

All Rights Reserved.

No part of this publication or the information in it may be quoted from or reproduced in any form by means such as printing, scanning, photocopying or otherwise without prior written permission of the copyright holder.

Disclaimer and Terms of Use:

Effort has been made to ensure that the information in this book is accurate and complete; however, the author and the publisher do not warrant the accuracy of the information text and graphics contained within the book due to the rapidly changing nature of science, research, known and unknown facts and internet. The Author and the publisher do not hold any responsibility for errors, omissions or contrary interpretation of the subject matter herein. This book is presented solely for Cooking and informational purposes only.

TABLE OF CONTENTS

- INTRODUCTION 8
- What Is Meal Prepping? 10
- Why Meal Prep? 11
- Benefits of Meal Prep 13
- The Healthy Meal Prep Cookbook Recipes: 16
  - Astonishing Chicken and Spinach Curry: 18
  - Simple Vegan Omelet: 19
  - Hawaiian Chicken Bowls: 21
  - Spiced Stir-fry Tofu: 23
  - Amazing Tray Baked Sea Bass and Veggies: 24
  - Homemade Granola Bars: 25
  - Chicken Nuggets: 27
  - Zucchini Pasta with Garlic and Oil: 28
  - Baker's Favorite Potato and chicken: 29
  - Sweet Potato Kale Hash: 30
  - Tangy Lemon Thyme Chicken: 31
  - Veggie Burgers: 32
  - Ultimate Chicken Kebobs with Lemony Goodness: 33
  - Savory Breakfast Muffins: 34
  - Chicken Fried Rice: 35
  - Potato and Spinach Gillette: 36
  - Avocado Salad with Blueberries and a Load of Chicken: 37
  - Bacon and Eggs: 38
  - Broccoli Rabe: 39
  - Vegetable Paella (Low Fat): 40
  - Himalayan Chicken Eggplant: 41

Freezer Breakfast Burritos: 42

Stew with Chicken and Vegetables: 43

Hot and Sour Chickpeas: 44

Authentic Tuna with Shaved Vegetables: 45

Yogurt and Granola Parfait: 46

Chicken Bruschetta: 47

Sweet and Sour Tofu: 48

Indian Lemon chicken Kabobs with Parsley Salad: 49

Beef and Vegetable Meatloaf: 50

Fried Catfish with Pickled peppers: 51

Lemon Brown Rice Pilaf: 52

Delightful and Authentic Shrimp Rolls: 53

Chicken Curry with Spinach: 54

Lamb Cutlets: 55

Lemon Garlic Chicken: 56

Nutty Squash and Eggs: 57

Ginger and Turmeric Grilled Chicken: 58

Cauliflower and Lentil Curry: 59

Chicken Vegetable bundles: 60

Ancient Fish Roast of the Greeks: 61

Kale Chickpea Mash: 62

Chicken with Broccoli: 63

Grilled Catfish Fillets with Tomato Salad: 64

Chicken and Herbal Pillared: 65

Hot Paprika Chicken Breast: 66

Risotto with Shrimps: 67

Asian Chicken Salad: 68

Authentic Spanish Gazpacho: 69

Coconut Chicken Curry: 70

- Chicken with Quinoa and Veggies: 71
- Quick Fry Chicken with Vegetable Rice: 72
- Very Worthy Fish Stew: 73
- Beef and Broccoli Stir Fry: 74
- Crusted Herb Pork Chops: 75
- Oatmeal-Crusted Chicken Wings and Veggies: 76
- Upbeat Spicy Pumpkin Chili: 77
- Chicken Taco Pizza: 78
- Easy Turkey Chili: 79
- Almond and Chicken Stir-Fry: 80
- Goat Cheese Herbal Pancake: 81
- Beef Taco Stuffed Avocadoes: 82
- Garlicky Lebanese Chicken Thighs: 83
- Classic Short Ribs with Olives: 84
- A very Grim and Brooding Blackened Chicken: 85
- Lamb Roast with Veggies: 86
- Beef Wrapped in Beef Fillet: 87
- Supremely Secret Wrap of Turkey and Bacon: 88
- Chicken parmesan: 89
- Chicken Mango and Cherry Tomato Salad: 90

CONCLUSION: 91

Other Books by Tanaya Hill 93

INTRODUCTION

Dear readers, this is Tanaya Hill! Firstly, thank and congratulate you for purchasing this book: **"The Healthy Meal Prep Cookbook: Make it Easy! Delicious and Simple Meals to Prep for Beginners."** Hope this book will be your best choice on amazon!

IS THERE ANYONE WHO ISN'T BUSY? For pretty much all time all of us, time is precious. I'm a mother of three kids. I run the household, work full-time and often myself shuttling the kids to school and activities. For years, getting healthy meals on the table was no easy feat. Before I got into the meal prepping groove, I spent too much time each day cooking, I was saddled with high food bills, and I watched a lot of food go to waste.

Since those days, I've learned that spending a few hours over the weekend planning meals, food shopping, and cooking is an incredible timesaver. I've been able to free myself of unnecessary stress, spend more time with my kids, reduce my grocery bill, and even find time to hit my favorite evening Pilate's class. But there was a learning curve.

When I first started meal prepping, I didn't always want to append time cooking during my precious weekend. I found it challenging to balance weekend activities with the planning and prepping of numerous meals. To make it more manageable, I started preparing only two or three meals and gradually worked my way up to about six. Some weekends I would cook three dishes, while on others I could prep six dishes, depending on my schedule. These days, sometimes I prep a double batch of certain dishes (like lasagna, meatballs, or soup), and freeze half for those weeks when I don't have time to prep. I've learned to build up my stash of frozen meals and balance it with just a few dishes I prep on Sunday__that's what I call smart meal prepping.

As a registered dietitian, I know that eating healthy is challenging. I wrote my first meal prep guide, **The Healthy Meal Prep Cookbook,** to show people just how easy it can be to prepare nutritious, ready-to-eat, portion-controlled meals. But I've come to realize that many people don't just want general guidance; they want specific, step-by-step instructions and meal prep plans that tell them what to eat and for which meal. While you're always welcome to tweak recipes and preps as you desire, this book was written to make sure you never have to do any guesswork as you begin to meal prep. Follow the cooking and storing instructions eat the meals on the days specified, and you'll succeed. It's as easy as that.

You can also gauge your individual needs and decide how many recipes you'll want to prepare for any given week. Whatever you choose, your end result will be a less stressful life filled with delicious, healthy and ready meals.

What Is Meal Prepping?

Meal prepping is the art of preparing your meals the night (or a few nights) before eating. It usually involves preparing a few portions of each Meal, packing them away in airtight containers, and storing in the fridge. Many people prep their meals these days, because it saves time, encourages healthy eating, and controls portions.

Sometimes, the meal is completely prepared and cooked in its entirety before being stacked away in the fridge or freezer until it is needed. Whereas sometimes, meals are only partially so they can be cooked right before eating. For example, you can prep lasagna by cooking the sauces and layering it all up before covering and storing in the fridge, raw. You would then place the lasagna into a preheated oven before eating the next night. Whatever prepping method you choose, its great way to manage your time and your diet!

Why Meal Prep?

There are countless reasons to get into the joys of meal prepping, but here are some of the reasons:

Saves time
By setting aside a chunk of time to get all or most of your meals for the week prepped, you are saving yourself hours of frazzled and rushed cooking throughout the coming days. You can wake up in the morning, grab your prepped breakfast from the fridge, and throw your prepped lunch into your bag (ready to eat as soon as you're ready!); and come home to a ready –made dinner you only need to heat in the oven or microwave. Not only do you save cooking time, you also save thinking time. I don't know about you, but thinking about what to have for breakfast, lunch and dinner always takes up far more of my time than it should!

Saves money
When you decide what to eat for lunch and dinner as you go through the week, you end up heading to the supermarket every couple of days, which increases your chance of spending money on things you don't really need. But when you make a plan of what you will eat for each meal for the entire week, you can do one shop where you buy only what you need for those particular meals. You will end up with far less unnecessary items and more money in your wallet!

Keeps you healthy with portion control and planning
Meal prepping is all about packing away single serving of food for each meal. Therefore, you only make enough for a certain number of portions, with no leftover, I'm sure you can sympathize with me when I say that leftovers are my absolute downfall! When I don't prep my meals, I end up eating far larger portions than I need, because it's right there in front of me! When you go to eat your breakfast, lunch and dinner, all you have to eat is the single portion you have made, nothing more.
Of course, this does means you need to prepare sensible portion size in the first place, which I have aimed to provide in these recipes. You can adjust the ingredient quantities to suit your personal portion-size preference for your BMI, calorie requirements and activity levels.

Helps you to reach your goals
Quite simply, prepping your meals helps you to remain in control of your eating habits in order to reach your weight loss and health-related goals. You can assess the calories and macros for each recipe and make sure they fit with your weight loss eating plan, so you know that each meal you enjoy is going to help you get to where you want to be.

Gives you some "you time"!
This work two ways! One: the actual meal-prepping process gives you some time for yourself to quietly potter away and enjoy being in the kitchen, with busy hands and lots of creating to do. Two: you will have so much more time to yourself (and for your loved ones) throughout the week when you would usually be rushing around trying to prepare meals from scratch.

Benefits of Meal Prep

The key to losing weight and staying healthy is to be prepared—prepare your mind and body! And the most important of all is to get started with weight loss meal prep! Tanaya Hill recommends you to do all your meal preps when you have free time so that you can have fresh homemade meals ready for the upcoming week.

Get geared up to prepare your meal with positive vibes by listening to your favorite music. It isn't really tough- all you have to do is organize your budget, your meals, buy raw ingredients in bulk and prepare everything in advance. Save money and loss weight!

You can spend few hours of your free time to prepare your meals, which will help you eliminate the stress of planning out your meals every day—especially when you are busy catching up with your hectic work schedule. Having your meal prepared beforehand will save you:

- ✓ **Time**

You can spend more time doing what you like to do instead of planning and cooking.

- ✓ **Money**

Cooking your own food saves money (in fact, a lot of money) when compared to buying meals from the restaurant.

- ✓ **Calories**

You are in control of your meal- you decide your calories, salt, oil in each and every meal.

- ✓ **Lucidity**

Preparing your meal in advance saves your brain space, i.e., you have one less thing (food) to worry about every day.

There are various benefits involved in meal prepping – you don't cheat (this is true!) when you spend your free time preparing meals, you are forced to buy stuff that is on your grocery list. This way you don't get tempted to buy deep-fried snacks or junk food.

You save money as your restaurant visits will considerably reduce, as there is a home cooked meal prepped and waiting for you. You don't have to rush home to prepare dinner or get up early to get your lunch and breakfast ready when your meal prep is already in place! As expected, you get time to work out or go for your early morning yoga classes! This will help you meet your fitness goals.

When you properly plan out meals much ahead of time, you get to learn portion control as well as fuel your body with nutritional food.

Maintaining a healthy lifestyle is not a tough task when you are committed to your mind and sketch out your planning well in advance. Get started by writing down the list of your favorite dishes (don't forget they should be healthy dishes). Prepare a meal plan for a week and get your shopping list ready.

Stock up on fresh vegetables and greens in your kitchen. Get started with chopping, roast then (if required as per your recipe), then go ahead with cooking (quinoa, rice or meat) and finally transfer them to airtight containers to refrigerate or freeze then. Your complete meal plan for the next 5 days is ready.

And most important, you'll become a meal prep master, with all its benefits:

- ✓ **Steady, satisfying weight loss-up to 5 pounds each week that you will keep off.**
- ✓ **Mastery of the simple skills of meal prepping.**
- ✓ **Automatic portion control-no counting calories, fat grams, carbohydrates, or any of that nonsense.**
- ✓ **Recipes for breakfast, lunch, dinner, and snacks so delicious you won't even know you're on a weight-loss plan.**
- ✓ **Control over what you put in your body.**
- ✓ **Meals that heal and renew your body, thanks to miracle nutrients rich in antioxidants and disease-fighting plant chemicals.**
- ✓ **An escape from emotional eating and bingeing.**
- ✓ **Stress free cooking and eating –and an overall stress-free lifestyle.**
- ✓ **More time and money to enjoy your life.**
- ✓ **Attainment of the weight, energy, and healthy you so want and deserve.**

By picking up this book and reading it, you are on your success. Every new bit of information you learn will help you create lasting habits. The meals in the book will nourish your body, and I promise you won't miss your old ways. Think of this book and its plan not as another diet, but as a new way of life.

Now that you have understood the theory of meal prep, let's move to the recipes segment and learn how to prep meals.

Welcome to the Healthy Meal Prep Cookbook!

The Healthy Meal Prep Cookbook Recipes:

Astonishing Chicken and Spinach Curry:

Serves: 4

Macros per serving:
Calories: 446
Protein: 33 grams
Fat: 3 grams
Carbohydrates: 39 grams

What you'll need:

- 1 pound of boneless and skinless Chicken thigh, cut into bite-sized pieces.
- 4 teaspoons of mild curry powder
- 1 tablespoon of coconut oil
- ½ of a finely chopped onion
- 1 tablespoon of minced and peeled ginger
- 3 minced cloves of garlic
- 1 cup of frozen peas
- 1 cup of cherry tomatoes
- 2/3 cup of low-sodium chicken broth
- ½ cup of full-fat coconut milk
- ½ teaspoon of sea salt
- 1 cup of quinoa
- 3 cups of baby spinach

How to make it:

1. In a medium sized bowl, add chicken and toss with curry powder until well-coated.
2. In a large sauté pan, heat oil over medium-high heat.
3. Add onions and sauté them for about 3 minutes until they are translucent.
4. Add ginger, seasoned chicken and garlic and sauté them for another 2 minutes until the chicken starts to show a nice brown exterior.
5. Reduce heat to low and partially cover the chicken.
6. Simmer for about 15 minutes.
7. In the meantime, cook quinoa according to package instructions.
8. Add ¼ teaspoon of salt to the quinoa and fluff it up using a fork. Cover it.
9. Add spinach to simmering curry about 1 minute before it is fully cooked and let it wilt.
10. Divide the curry into 4 portions and serve over quinoa.

Simple Vegan Omelet:

Serves: 2

Macros per serving:
Calories: 232
Protein: 22 grams
Fat: 7.8 grams
Carbohydrates: 22 grams

What you'll need:

For Omelet:
- 10 ounces firm silken tofu, drained, pat dried
- 4 large cloves garlic, minced
- 4 tablespoons nutritional yeast
- ½ teaspoon paprika
- Pepper to taste
- Salt to taste
- 2 teaspoons cornstarch
- 4 tablespoons hummus
- 1 teaspoons olive oil

For the filling:
- 2½ cups vegetables of your choice
- 2 teaspoons olive oil
- Salt to taste
- Pepper to taste

To serve:
- 2-3 tablespoons olive oil
- Salsa as required
- A handful fresh herbs, chopped
- ½ cup vegan parmesan cheese, shredded

How to make it:

1. For the omelet batter. Place a heatproof skillet over medium heat. Add oil. When the oil is heated, add garlic and sauté' until light brown.
2. Remove from heat and add the sautéed garlic into a blender. Add rest of the ingredients of the omelet into the blender and blend until smooth. Add a little water if required and blend again. The batter should not be very thick. So add water accordingly. Transfer into an airtight container and refrigerate until use.
3. For the filling: Place the same skillet back on heat. Add oil. When the oil id heated, add vegetables, salt and pepper and sauté until tender. Remove from heat and set aside in the refrigerator in an airtight in an airtight container until use.

4. To use: remove both the containers from the refrigerator 30 minutes before making the omelet.
5. Place a medium size ovenproof nonstick pan over medium heat. Add about tablespoon oil. Swirl the pan so that the oil spreads all over the skillet.
6. When the oil is heated, pour half the omelet batter onto the pan. Swirl the pan so that the batter spreads or spread with the back of spoon carefully.
7. Cook until the edges are getting to be dry. Remove the pan from heat and place in an oven.
8. Bake in a preheated oven at 375^0 F for about 10-15 minutes until brown-golden brown (as per your choice). Keep a check on the omelet after about 10 minutes of cooking.
9. Remove from the oven and spread half the vegetables on it. Bake for a couple of minutes. Gently slide a spatula below the omelet to loosen it. Top with a little salsa, herbs and cheese and fold over. Carefully slide on to a plate and serve.
10. Repeat steps 6-9 to make the other omelet.

Hawaiian Chicken Bowls:

Serves: 4

Macros per serving:
Calories: 342
Protein: 29 grams
Fat: 7 grams
Carbohydrates: 69 grams

What you'll need:

- 4 cups rice noodles, cooked
- 1 cup pineapple, fresh and cubed
- ½ cup pineapple juice
- 4 small chicken breasts, skinless and boneless
- 2 tablespoons ketchup
- 1 teaspoon garlic, minced
- ½ teaspoon ginger, fresh and grated
- 2 tablespoons tamari, low sodium
- 1 tablespoon honey, raw
- Coconut chips to taste
- Green onion, diced for garnish
- Sea salt to taste

Pineapple Stir Fry:
- 1 tablespoon coconut oil
- 1 cup purple onion, diced
- 2 sweet peppers, large and diced
- 2 cups kale, chopped and packed
- 1 tablespoon pineapple juice
- 1 tablespoon chili sauce
- 1 tablespoon tamari, low sodium
- ½ tablespoon honey, raw
- 1 tablespoon garlic, minced

How to make it:

1. Get out a bowl and whisk your ketchup, ginger, garlic, pineapple juice, honey, salt and tamari together. Put your chicken breasts into a crock pot, and pour the sauce over it.
2. Cook your chicken for one and a half to two hours on high, and then shred it.
3. Heat a tablespoon of your coconut oil in a skillet, adding in your pepper and onions. Sauté until your onions turn translucent, and then add in your kale. Sauté or a few more minutes until wilted.
4. Mix the rest of your ingredients in a bowl, pouring it over your stir fry. Cook for a few minutes. Your sauce should reduce, and then you're ready to assemble your bowls.
5. Add your noodles to the bottom, and top with your pineapple. Add your shredded chicken next.
6. Place your pineapple stir fry on top, and then sprinkle in your green onions and coconut chips.

Spiced Stir-fry Tofu:

Serves: 4

Macros per serving:
Calories: 134
Protein: 12 grams
Fat: 0 grams
Carbohydrates: 0 grams

What you'll need:

- 2 teaspoons ground cumin
- 1 tablespoon paprika
- 1 teaspoon ground ginger
- Pinch of cayenne pepper
- 1 tablespoon coconut palm sugar
- 1 bog block tofu, cubed
- 2 tablespoons olive oil
- 2 garlic cloves, crushed
- 1 bunch spring onions, sliced
- 1 red pepper, sliced
- 3 cups brown cap mushrooms, quartered
- 1 yellow pepper, sliced
- 1 courgette, sliced
- 1 cup green beans, halved
- 1½ cups pine nuts
- 1 tablespoon lime juice, freshly squeezed
- 1 tablespoon coconut sugar
- Pinch of salt
- Pinch of ground black pepper

How to make it:

1. In a bowl, combine paprika, cayenne, cumin, and sugar. Season with salt and pepper. Coat the tofu cubes in the mixture.
2. Meanwhile, heat the pan. Pour olive oil. Cook tofu cubes over high heat for 4 minutes. Turn occasionally, taking care not to break the tofu.
3. Remove cooked tofu and drain in kitchen paper. Set aside.
4. Heat the remaining oil. Sauté onions and garlic for 3 minutes. Tip in courgette, mushrooms, red peppers, yellow pepper, and beans.
5. Toss well to combine cook for 6 minutes or until the vegetables are tender, season with salt and pepper.
6. Return tofu in the pan. Scatter pine nuts, honey, and lime juice. Stir well. Serve.

Amazing Tray Baked Sea Bass and Veggies:

Serves: 2

Macros per serving:
Calories: 387
Protein: 28 grams
Fat: 17 grams
Carbohydrates: 28 grams

What you'll need:

- 300g of red-skinned potatoes thinly sliced into rounds
- 1 red pepper cut into strips
- 2 tablespoons of extra virgin olive oil
- 1 sprig of fresh rosemary, leaves removed and chopped very finely
- 2 sea bass fillets
- 25g of halved, pitted black olives
- ½ lemon sliced into thin rounds
- A handful of basil leaves, chopped

How to make it:

1. Pre-heat oven to 350° F.
2. In a baking dish, arrange pepper and potato slices.
3. Drizzle with about 1 tablespoon of oil and scatter with rosemary
4. Season with pepper and salt to taste.
5. Toss everything well and roast for about 25 minutes, turning about halfway through.
6. Arrange the fillets on top of potatoes and peppers, and scatter with olives.
7. Add lemon slices and drizzle with remaining oil.
8. Roast for about 8 minutes and serve with a garnish of basil.

Homemade Granola Bars:

Serves: 32

Macros per serving:
Calories: 262
Protein: 7 grams
Fat: 16 grams
Carbohydrates: 24 grams

What you'll need:

- 4 cups old fashioned rolled oats
- 1 cup shredded coconut, unsweetened
- 2/3 cup honey
- 4 teaspoons vanilla extract
- 1 cup wheat germ, toasted
- 2/3 cup maple syrup
- ½ teaspoon salt
- ½ cup walnuts, chopped into small pieces
- ½ cup almonds, chopped into small pieces
- ½ cup pecans, chopped into small pieces
- ½ cup cashew, chopped into small pieces
- ½ cup dried cranberries, chopped into small pieces
- 1 cup raisins, chopped into small pieces
- ½ cup dried cherries, chopped into small pieces
- ½ cup dried blueberries, chopped into small pieces
- ½ cup dried apricots, chopped into small pieces

How to make it:

1. Line a large baking dish or 2 smaller baking dishes with parchment paper. Grease it with butter. Set aside.
2. Spread oats and all the nuts on a rimmed baking sheet.
3. Bake in a preheated oven at 300^0 F for 10 minutes. Stir after 5 minutes of baking. Keep a check on the oven so that you don't end up with burnt stuff.
4. Remove from the oven and transfer into a large bowl. Let it cool for 10 minutes.
5. Add rest of the ingredients and stir until well combined.

6. Transfer the entire contents into the prepared baking dish. Spread it all over the dish with a spatula. Press it down tightly to the bottom of the pan else it will break after baking.
7. Bake in a preheated oven at 300^0 F for about 25 minutes or until golden brown.
8. Remove from the oven and cool completely.
9. Chop into 32 squares. Place them in an airtight container or in a zip lock container in the freezer until use.

Chicken Nuggets:

Serves: 5

Macros per serving:
Calories: 240
Protein: 21 grams
Fat: 3 grams
Carbohydrates: 32 grams

What you'll need:

- 1½ kg of chicken
- 200 grams of flour
- 200 grams of cornflakes
- 5 eggs
- 1 tablespoon of paprika

How to make it:

1. Cut the meat into small pieces about 3-5 cm long. After grinding the cornflakes in a in a blender.
2. Mix the flour and paprika in a separate bowl. Also, whisk eggs separately.
3. Each piece of the chicken dip in flour, then in eggs and finally, in flakes. Do this carefully if you want the nuggets to be crispy.
4. Cover the baking tray with parchment and put the breaded chicken pieces on it. Bake the nuggets in the oven at 180^0 C for 15-20 minutes.
5. When the nuggets cool down, place them in a sealed plastic bag and put them in the freezer.
6. Don't forget to glue the label. Indicate the name of the dish and the date of preparation.
7. When necessary, take the nuggets, and reheat in the microwave and enjoy an excellent dish. Bon Appetite!

Zucchini Pasta with Garlic and Oil:

Serves: 4

Macros per serving:
Calories: 93.8
Protein: 3.4 grams
Fat: 4.8 grams
Carbohydrates: 11.5 grams

What you'll need:

- Zucchini pasta
- 5 tablespoons extra virgin olive oil
- 4 garlic cloves, crushed
- 1 dried red chili
- 1 handful fresh flat parsley, roughly chopped
- Pinch of salt

How to make it:

1. Pour water onto the pan just enough to let the zucchini pasta with salted water to boil for 5 minutes.
2. Meanwhile, heat the olive oil in the pan over low heat.
3. Add garlic and dried chili over low heat or until the garlic is turning brown.
4. Discard chili. Reserve some for garnish.
5. Drain pasta and transfer in a bowl.
6. Drizzle in olive oil. Put the garlic mixture. Garnish with parsley and chili. Serve.

Baker's Favorite Potato and chicken:

Serves: 4

Macros per serving:
Calories: 323
Protein: 22 grams
Fat: 15 grams
Carbohydrates: 23 grams

What you'll need:

- 4 boneless chicken breasts, skin on
- 3 tablespoons of olive oil
- 500g of fresh potatoes
- 140g of large pitted olives
- 1 quartered lemon
- 8 fresh bay leaves
- 6 unpeeled garlic cloves
- Lettuce leaves

How to make it:

1. Pre-heat oven to 350^0 F.
2. Toss potatoes, olives, bay leaves, lemon quarters and garlic with oil.
3. Place 5 garlic cloves and remaining ingredients in a roasting pan with chicken skin side up.
4. Cook for 60 minutes.
5. Check the potatoes for tenderness. If they are not tender enough and the chicken is not crispy, cook for another 15 minutes.
6. Place the chicken and potatoes on a serving plate.
7. In a bowl mash remaining garlic clove with the back of a spoon (discard the skin of the clove first).
8. Mix the mashed garlic with meat juices from the pan and serve the chicken and potatoes on lettuce and a drizzle of meat juice.

Sweet Potato Kale Hash:

Serves: 8

Macros per serving:
Calories: 247
Protein: 16 grams
Fat: 12 grams
Carbohydrates: 5 grams

What you'll need:

- 4 tablespoons extra virgin olive oil
- 2 large sweet potatoes, peeled, cubed
- 1 yellow onion, finely chopped
- 2 red bell peppers, finely chopped
- 8 cups kale, discard hard ribs and stems, torn
- 2 tablespoons garlic, minced
- 8 chicken sausages, precooked, sliced
- 4 tablespoons balsamic vinegar
- Salt and pepper to taste

How to make it:

1. Place a skillet over medium heat. Add oil. When the oil is heated, add onions, sweet potatoes, pepper and sauté until the onions turn translucent.
2. Add kale and sauté until kale wilts. Sprinkle salt, pepper and vinegar. Mix well.
3. Serve if desired. Store the remaining hash in an airtight container in the refrigerator. It can last for 2-3 days.
4. Remove from the oven and heat thoroughly before serving.

Tangy Lemon Thyme Chicken:

Serves: 4

Macros per serving:
Calories: 289
Protein: 25 grams
Fat: 4 grams
Carbohydrates: 3 grams

What you'll need:

- 1 teaspoon thyme
- 1 teaspoon salt
- ½ teaspoon pepper
- 1-zest lemon
- 2-juice lemons
- 4 chicken breast

How to make it:

1. Start out by heating your oven to 375° F.
2. While this is warming up, take a small bowl and mix together your lemon zest, lemon juice, salt, pepper, and the thyme.
3. When you are ready, place the chicken breast into the bottom of a baking dish and pour the lemon mixture over the top.
4. Be sure to swirl the dish around to assure the chicken is completely coated.
5. Finally, pop the dish into the oven for forty minutes or so. When it is cooked through, the juices will run clear.
6. Once cooked, remove from the oven, cool, and portion on breast per container. For a well-rounded meal, pair with a favorite.

Veggie Burgers:

Serves: 4

Macros per serving:
Calories: 124
Protein: 10.9 grams
Fat: 4.4 grams
Carbohydrates: 9.9 grams

What you'll need:

- 1 ½ cups mushrooms, finely chopped
- 1 carrot, chopped
- 1 courgette, chopped
- ¼ cup peanuts, unsalted
- 1 onion , chopped
- 2 cups breadcrumbs
- 2 tablespoons fresh parsley, chopped
- 1 teaspoon yeast extract
- Oatmeal, for shaping
- Pinch of salt and black pepper

How to make it:

1. In a pan, cook mushrooms for 10 minutes. Don't put oil.
2. This is so you can drive off the excess moisture in the mushrooms.
3. Meanwhile, in a food processor, combine carrots, courgette, peanuts, and onion.
4. Processes until all ingredients are well combined.
5. Tip in yeast extract, cooked mushrooms, breadcrumbs, and parsley. Season with salt and pepper.
6. Coat your hands with oatmeal, shape mixture into burgers, place inside the fridge for 30 minutes.
7. Once ready to cook, heat the olive oil in a pan.
8. Cook burger patties for 8 minutes or until golden brown. Serve.

Ultimate Chicken Kebobs with Lemony Goodness:

Serves: 4

Macros per serving:
Calories: 311
Protein: 38 grams
Fat: 14.39 grams
Carbohydrates: 6 grams

What you'll need:

- 3 tablespoons of fresh lemon juice, divided
- 1 tablespoon of minced garlic, divided
- 1½ teaspoon of dried oregano, divided
- ¾ teaspoon of kosher salt, divided
- ¾ teaspoon of freshly ground black pepper divided
- 3 tablespoons extra virgin olive oil, divided
- 6 ounces of boneless and skinless chicken breast cut into 1½-inch cubes
- 2 cups of fresh parsley leaves
- 1 cup of chopped cherry tomatoes
- 1 tablespoon of torn fennel fronds

How to make it:

1. In a bowl, mix 2 tablespoons of juice, 2 teaspoons of garlic, ½ teaspoon of salt, and 1 teaspoon of oregano and ½ teaspoon of pepper.
2. Add 1 tablespoon of oil and whisk
3. Add the chicken and stir well.
4. Marinate for about 2 hours in fridge
5. Remove the chicken from bowl and discard the marinade.
6. With 10-inch skewers, skewer chicken.
7. Place a grill pan over high heat.
8. Add the skewers and cook for about 6 minutes or until they are done.
9. In a medium bowl and mix 1 tablespoon of juice, ½ teaspoon of oregano, ½ teaspoon of garlic, 1 teaspoon of pepper and ¼ teaspoon of salt.
10. Slowly add the rest of the oil and whisk well.
11. Add tomatoes, fennel and parsley. Toss everything well.
12. Serve the chicken over prepared salad

Savory Breakfast Muffins:

Serves: 24

Macros per serving:
Calories: 231
Protein: 9 grams
Fat: 9 grams
Carbohydrates: 29 grams

What you'll need:

- 12 large eggs
- 1 cup cheddar cheese, shredded
- 1 cup red bell pepper, chopped
- ½ cup Canadian bacon, chopped
- ½ cup fresh parsley, chopped
- 2/3 cup old fashioned oats
- 2 cups flour
- 2 tablespoons baking powder
- ½ teaspoon ground cinnamon
- 1 teaspoon salt or to taste
- ½ teaspoon pepper or to taste
- ½ cup applesauce, unsweetened

How to make it:

1. Whisk together in a bowl, eggs and applesauce until well incorporated.
2. Add all the dry ingredients into a bowl and mix well. Pour the egg mixture into the bowl of dry ingredients and mix until well incorporated.
3. Add cheese, bacon, bell pepper and parsley and stir.
4. Grease 2 muffin pans (12 muffins each) with nonstick cooking spray. Pour the batter into the muffin pans (fill up to 2/3).
5. Place the muffin tins in a preheated oven. Bake at 375^0 F for 15-20 minutes or until a toothpick when inserted in the center comes out clean.
6. Remove from the oven and place on a wire a knife and invert on to a plate. Serve.
7. To store: Wrap each muffin with plastic wrap and place in a freezer bag or airtight container. Place in the freezer until use.
8. To use: remove from the freezer, discard the plastic wrap and wrap it in a paper towel.
9. Microwave on high for 30-45 seconds and serve.

Chicken Fried Rice:

Serves: 6

Macros per serving:
Calories:
Protein: grams
Fat: grams
Carbohydrates: grams

What you'll need:

- ½ tablespoon sesame oil
- 6 cups rice, cooked
- 3 cups mixed vegetables, frozen
- 1 lb. chicken, cooked and cubed
- 5 eggs, beaten
- 1/3 cup soy sauce
- Black pepper to taste
- Vegetable oil as needed

How to make it:

1. Start by heating your oil in a skillet, scrambling your eggs. Set your now scrambled eggs to the side.
2. Add in your sesame oil to the same pan, add toss in your chicken. Cook for about four minutes.
3. Next, stir in your soy sauce and mixed vegetables. You'll want to cook until your vegetables are tender, and then season with black pepper.
4. Mix everything together, and allow it to cool before portioning it out to freeze.

Potato and Spinach Gillette:

Serves: 6

Macros per serving:
Calories: 262
Protein: 3.3 grams
Fat: 18.4 grams
Carbohydrates: 22.9 grams

What you'll need:

- 2 lbs large potatoes, peeled, slice thinly after boiling
- 1 lb. fresh spinach
- 1½ cups low fat cream cheese
- 2 eggs
- 1 tablespoon mustard
- Fresh chives, chopped
- Pinch of salt
- Pinch of pepper
- Salad greens

How to make it:

1. Preheat the oven to 350^0 F. Line a round cake tin with baking paper.
2. Put potatoes in a pan. Cover with cold water. Bring to a boil and cook for 10 minutes. Drain potatoes. Allow the cooked potatoes to cool before slicing.
3. Place spinach in a pan with water. Cover and cook on low until then spinach wilts. Drain well and squeeze out excess moisture. Finely chop spinach.
4. Meanwhile out together cream cheese, eggs, and mustard. Add in spinach and chives.
5. In the lined tin, layer the potatoes in circles. Top potatoes with cream cheese mixture. Cover the cake tin with foil. Place inside the roasting tin.
6. Fill roasting tin with boiling water. Cook inside the oven for 40 minutes. Transfer to a serving plate with salad greens.

Avocado Salad with Blueberries and a Load of Chicken:

Serves: 2

Macros per serving:
Calories: 402
Protein: 34 grams
Fat: 19 grams
Carbohydrates: 18 grams

What you'll need:

- 1 clove of garlic, chopped
- 85g of blueberries
- 1 tablespoon of extra virgin rapeseed oil
- 2 teaspoons of balsamic vinegar
- 125g of fresh baby broad beans
- 1 large cooked and finely chopped beet
- 1 stoned, peeled and sliced avocado
- 85g mixed baby lettuce
- 175g of cooked chicken

How to make it:

1. In a large bowl, mash garlic, half of the blueberries and oil.
2. Add vinegar and season with black pepper.
3. Boil beans for about 5 minutes until they are tender.
4. Drain, making sure to leave them un-skinned.
5. Pile warm beans on top of the dressing with the rest of the blueberries.
6. Add avocado, beet, lettuce and chicken.
7. Toss everything well and spoon into serving bowls.

Bacon and Eggs:

Serves: 2

Macros per serving:
Calories: 272
Protein: 15 grams
Fat: 22 grams
Carbohydrates: 1 gram

What you'll need:

- 4 eggs
- 1 cup spinach, finely shredded
- ½ cup cheese or to taste, shredded + extra to top
- 1 cup bacon, cooked, crumbled
- Salt to taste
- Pepper to taste

How to make it:

1. Mix together the eggs, spinach, cheese, salt and pepper in a large bowl.
2. Pour into masons jar.
3. Microwave on high for 1 ½ to 2 minutes. Check it between if it is set.
4. When done, remove from the microwave.
5. Top with bacon and extra cheese if you desire.
6. Tightly screw the lids.
7. Store in the refrigerator until use.
8. To use: Remove the jars from the refrigerator, uncover the jar.
9. Heat in the microwave for 40-50 seconds and serve.

Broccoli Rabe:

Serves: 4

Macros per serving:
Calories: 192
Protein: 4.5 grams
Fat: 17.2 grams
Carbohydrates: 5.2 grams

What you'll need:

- 1 pound broccoli Rabe
- 5 tablespoons olive oil
- 1 garlic clove
- 1 tablespoons parmesan cheese
- Salt to taste

How to make it:

1. Fill a pot with water and salt and add the trimmed broccoli and boil to make the broccoli tender.
2. In another pan, heat the olive oil and fry the garlic.
3. Add in the broccoli rabe and fry for 10 minutes.
4. Sprinkle parmesan cheese and serve!

Vegetable Paella (Low Fat):

Serves: 6

Macros per serving:
Calories: 453
Protein: 13.5 grams
Fat: 3.7 grams
Carbohydrates: 96.3 grams

What you'll need:

- 2 garlic cloves, crushed
- 1 onion, chopped
- 1 red pepper, sliced
- 2 celery sticks, chopped
- Leeks, sliced
- 2 cups cap mushrooms, sliced
- 2 courgettes, sliced
- 2 cups brown rice
- 1½ cups peas
- 4 tablespoons dry white wine
- 2 cups vegetable stock
- 1 can cannellini beans
- Saffron strands
- 3 tablespoons fresh mixed herbs, chopped
- Pinch of salt
- Pinch of ground pepper
- Lemon wedges, for garnish

How to make it:

1. In a large pan, put together garlic, onion, red pepper, celery, leeks, mushrooms, and courgettes.
2. Add in rice, peas, wine, vegetable stock, beans, and saffron.
3. Bring mixture to a boil.
4. Stir continuously and reduce heat.
5. Allow to simmer for 30 minutes or until the liquid has been absorbed and the rice cooked.
6. Stir in herbs and tomatoes.
7. Season with salt and pepper.
8. Garnish with lemon wedges. Serve.

Himalayan Chicken Eggplant:

Serves: 4

Macros per serving:
Calories: 229
Protein: 27 grams
Fat: 9 grams
Carbohydrates: 7 grams

What you'll need:

- 1 large eggplant
- 2 tablespoons of extra virgin olive oil
- ¾ pound of organic chicken breast cut into small cubes
- 1 chopped onion
- 2 crushed garlic cloves
- 1 cup of chopped mushrooms
- 2 cups of fresh spinach
- 1 can of diced tomatoes
- 2 tablespoons of mina harissa sauce
- 1 tablespoon of fresh basil
- 1 teaspoon of garlic granules
- Himalayan salt
- Red pepper flakes

How to make it:

1. Pre-heat oven to 375° F.
2. Slice eggplant in half, scoop out the center and brush with olive oil.
3. Bake for about 15 minutes until tender. Cool and chop.
4. Heat 1 tablespoon of oil in a skillet.
5. Sauté garlic briefly.
6. Add the chopped onion, mushrooms, chicken and chopped eggplant.
7. Cook until the chicken is opaque.
8. Add the spices, harissa and tomatoes.
9. Add the spinach and mix everything until cooked.
10. Add the mixture into scooped out eggplant skin and bake for another 10 minutes. Serve!

Freezer Breakfast Burritos:

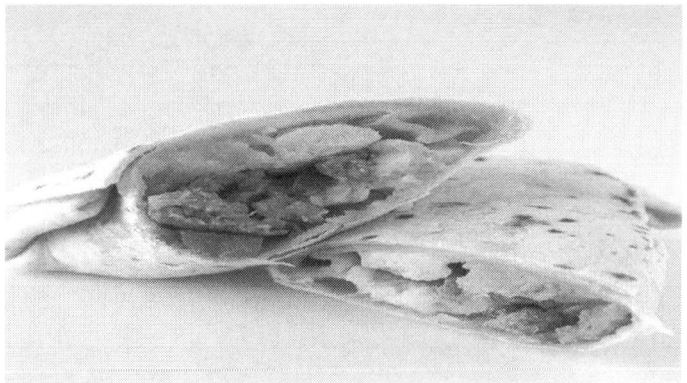

Serves: 8

Macros per serving:
Calories: 401
Protein: 17.6 grams
Fat: 23.5 grams
Carbohydrates: 30.1 grams

What you'll need:

- 16 large eggs
- 2 tablespoons extra virgin olive oil
- 2 red peppers, finely minced
- 2 tablespoons garlic, minced
- 1 red onion, finely minced
- 8 pieces thick cut bacon, cooked until crisp
- 8 multigrain or whole wheat tortillas
- Salt to taste
- Pepper to taste
- 2-3 tablespoons milk

How to make it:

1. Whisk together eggs and milk in a bowl.
2. Place a saucepan over medium heat. Add oil. When the oil is heated, add garlic and sauté until fragrant.
3. Add onion and red pepper and sauté until onions are translucent. Pour the egg mixture and sauté until it is cooked. Remove from heat.
4. Place the tortillas on your work area. Divide the egg mixture between the tortillas. Place a piece of bacon over it. Sprinkle Cheese. Wrap tightly.
5. Warp the burrito first in max paper and then in foil. Place in the freezer. It can last for 1 month in the freezer.
6. To use: Unwrap the burrito and place on a microwave safe plate. Microwave for 2-3 minutes. Turn the burrito once half way through heating.
7. Remove from the microwave and serve after a minute.

Stew with Chicken and Vegetables:

Serves: 9

Macros per serving:
Calories: 360
Protein: 28 grams
Fat: 8 grams
Carbohydrates: 40 grams

What you'll need:

- 1 kg of chicken fillet
- 2 sweet peppers
- 1 onion
- 2 cloves garlic
- 1 tablespoon of honey
- 1 tablespoon of apple cider vinegar
- 1 tablespoon of chili powder
- 2 teaspoons of cumin
- 1 teaspoon of paprika

How to make it:

1. Chop the chicken with straw. Remove seeds from pepper and cut.
2. Peel and chop onion and garlic. Use the package with zip lock.
3. Put in it all the ingredients, including honey and apple cider vinegar. Pump the air out of the bag. Freeze.
4. When necessary, unfreeze the bag. Content place in the multicore and cook the stew for 3-6 hours.
5. You can all the manipulations in the morning, so that in the evening when you come home from work, you can enjoy a delicious dinner. Bon Appetite!

Hot and Sour Chickpeas:

Serves: 4

Macros per serving:
Calories: 508
Protein: 17.5 grams
Fat: 12.6 grams
Carbohydrates: 85.8 grams

What you'll need:

- Tablespoons olive oil
- 2 onions, finely chopped
- 2 tomatoes, finely chopped
- 1 tablespoons ground cumin
- 1 tablespoon ground coriander
- 1 teaspoon ground cinnamon
- 1 teaspoon ground fenugreek
- 1 can chickpeas, drained
- 2 cups vegetable stock
- 2 hot green chilies, thinly sliced
- 1 fresh root ginger, grated
- 4 tablespoons lemon juice, freshly squeezed
- Pinch of salt
- 1 tablespoon fresh coriander, chopped

How to make it:

1. Heat the olive oil in a casserole. Sauté onions and reserve some for later. Cook for 4 minutes or until browned.
2. Add in tomatoes and mash to a pulp.
3. Tip in ground cumin, coriander, cinnamon, and fenugreek. Stir in chickpeas and vegetable stock.
4. Season with salt and pepper. Cook for 20 minutes.
5. Add more water if it becomes too dry.
6. Meanwhile, in a small bowl, put together reserved onions, ginger, chilies, and lemon juice.
7. Pour mixture on the chickpeas. Garnish with coriander. Serve.

Authentic Tuna with Shaved Vegetables:

Serves: 4

Macros per serving:
Calories: 366
Protein: 43 grams
Fat: 15 grams
Carbohydrates: 12 grams

What you'll need:

- ¼ cup of extra virgin olive oil, divided
- 1 tablespoon of rice vinegar
- 1 teaspoon of kosher salt, divided
- ¾ teaspoon of Dijon mustard
- ¾ teaspoon of honey
- 4 ounces of thinly shaved baby gold beets
- 4 ounces of trimmed and shaved fennel bulb
- 4 ounces of thinly shaved baby turnips
- 6 ounce of very thinly sliced Granny Smith apple
- 2 teaspoons of toasted sesame seeds
- 6 ounces of tuna steaks
- ½ teaspoon of black pepper
- 1 tablespoon of torn fennel fronds

How to make it:

1. In a large bowl, mix 2 tablespoons of oil, ½ teaspoon of salt, vinegar, honey and mustard.
2. Add fennel, apple, beets and turnip.
3. Toss everything well to ensure that they are well coated.
4. Sprinkle with sesame seeds and again.
5. Place a cast-iron skillet over high heat.
6. Add 2 tablespoons of oil.
7. Season tuna with ½ teaspoon of salt and pepper.
8. Cook tuna about 90 seconds on each side.
9. Remove and slice the tuna.
10. Serve with fennel mixture.

Yogurt and Granola Parfait:

Serves: 3

Macros per serving:
Calories: 402
Protein: 7 grams
Fat: 15 grams
Carbohydrates: 66 grams

What you'll need:

- 2 cups plain, low fat yogurt
- 2 cups fruits or berries of your choice
- ¼ cup honey
- ¾ cup rolled oats
- ¼ cup nuts, chopped and seeds of your choice
- ½ tablespoon olive oil
- ½ teaspoon cinnamon
- ¼ teaspoon vanilla extract
- A pinch of salt

How to make it:

1. Grease a baking dish with cooking spray or butter and set aside.
2. Mix together the oats, nuts, oil, cinnamon, vanilla, salt and 2 tablespoons honey. Mix until well coated.
3. Spread evenly on a greased baking dish.
4. Bake for around 45 minutes, stirring it every 15 minutes.
5. The granola should be golden brown in color when it is ready. Otherwise bake for another 10-15 minutes or until done.
6. Take 3 masons jars. Divide and spoon yogurt in it, divide and pour the remaining honey over it.
7. Next layer it with half the fruits and followed by half the granola.
8. Repeat the above layer. Tightly screw on the lids and refrigerate.
9. It can store up to 3 days. Serve either cold or at room temperature.

Chicken Bruschetta:

Serves: 4

Macros per serving:
Calories: 330
Protein: 28 grams
Fat: 4 grams
Carbohydrates: 8 grams

What you'll need:

- .25 cup basil
- .10 teaspoon salt
- 1 teaspoon balsamic vinegar
- 1 teaspoon olive oil
- .50 red onion
- 1 garlic
- 5 tomatoes
- 4 chicken breast

How to make it:

1. Begin by heating your oven to 375^0 F.
2. If you desire, season the chicken breast with salt and pepper before popping it onto a baking sheet.
3. Place the chicken in the oven for about forty minutes.
4. While the chicken bakes, take a small bowl and mix together your basil, balsamic vinegar, olive oil, onion, garlic, and the chopped tomatoes.
5. Finally, remove your chicken from the oven and allow cooling. Portion out your chicken into your containers, and you have a very healthy lunch or dinner.

Sweet and Sour Tofu:

Serves: 2

Macros per serving:
Calories: 400
Protein: 33.5 grams
Fat: 76.2 grams
Carbohydrates: 130 grams

What you'll need:

- ½ tablespoon coconut oil
- 1 firm tofu, sliced into strips
- 1 onion, chopped
- 1 garlic clove, minced
- 1 red pepper, chopped
- 1 green pepper, chopped
- 1 cup brown rice, cooked

For the Sauce:

- 1/3 cup pineapple chunks, reserve juice
- 3 tablespoons brown rice vinegar
- 2 tablespoons tomato paste
- ½ tablespoon tamari
- ½ tablespoon water
- ½ tablespoon corn starch

How to make it:

1. In a small bowl, combine cornstarch and water. Set aside.
2. Meanwhile, in a saucepan, put together tomato paste, pineapple chunks with juice, and vinegar. Allow to simmer for 10 minutes.
3. Add in cornstarch. Stir well until the sauce thickens.
4. Meanwhile, preheat the broiler. Prepare a baking pan lined with baking sheet.
5. Dip tofu in the sauce. Line in a baking sheet. Broil for 5 minutes, flip to make sure all sides are coated well. Continue broiling for 5 more minutes.
6. In a pan, pour coconut oil. Sauté onion, garlic, and bell pepper for 3 minutes or until softened. Set aside.
7. Serve by placing broiled tofu on top of bed of greens or rice. Pt. sautéed veggies on the side.

Indian Lemon chicken Kabobs with Parsley Salad:

Serves: 4

Macros per serving:
Calories: 311
Protein: 38 grams
Fat: 14.39 grams
Carbohydrates: 6 grams

What you'll need:

- 3 tablespoons of fresh lemon juice, divided
- 1 tablespoon of minced garlic, divided
- ½ teaspoon of dried oregano, divided
- ¾ teaspoon of kosher salt, divided
- ¾ teaspoon of freshly ground black pepper, divided
- 3 tablespoons of extra virgin olive oil, divided
- 6 ounces of boneless and skinless chicken breast, cut into 1½ inch cubes.
- 2 cups of fresh parsley leaves
- 1 cup of chopped cherry tomatoes
- 1 tablespoon of torn fennel fronds

How to make it:

1. In a bowl, mix 2 tablespoons of juice, 2 teaspoons of garlic, ½ teaspoon of salt, and 1 teaspoon of orange and ½ teaspoon of pepper.
2. Whisk in 1 tablespoon of oil.
3. Add the chicken and stir well.
4. Let it marinate for about 2 hours in the fridge.
5. Remove the chicken from the bowl and discard the marinade.
6. Load chicken chunks on 10-inch skewers. Heat grill on high.
7. Cook skewers for about 6 minutes or until they are done.
8. In a medium bowl, mix 1 tablespoon of juice, ½ teaspoon of oregano, and ½ teaspoon of garlic, ¼ teaspoon of pepper and ¼ teaspoon of salt.
9. Slowly add the rest of the oil and whisk well.
10. Add tomatoes and parsley. Toss everything well.
11. Serve the chicken on top of the prepared salad.

Beef and Vegetable Meatloaf:

Serves: 4

Macros per serving:
Calories: 223
Protein: 37 grams
Fat: 24.2 grams
Carbohydrates: 39.2 grams

What you'll need:

- 1 lb. ground beef
- 1 onion, diced
- 1 carrot, grated
- 1 cup brown rice, cooked
- 1 zucchini, grated
- 1 egg, beaten
- 1 tablespoon tamari
- ¾ cup Greek yogurt, plain
- 2 tablespoons parsley, fresh and chopped
- 1 teaspoon ground black pepper

How to make it:

1. Start by heating your oven to 360^0 F. and then grease a loaf pan.
2. In a bowl, combine all ingredients, mixing them well.
3. Place the mixture in your pan baking for an hour.
4. Let it stand for ten minutes before portioning it out to freeze it. Make sure it's cooled down before you freeze it!

Fried Catfish with Pickled peppers:

Serves: 6

Macros per serving:
Calories: 507
Protein: 29.4 grams
Fat: 23.8 grams
Carbohydrates: 43 grams

What you'll need:

- 1½ cups all-purpose flour
- 2¼ teaspoons table salt
- 2 teaspoons freshly ground black pepper
- 4 large eggs
- 1½ cups plain yellow cornmeal
- 4 (6-OZ.) catfish fillets
- Vegetable oil
- Pickled peppers

How to make it:

1. Combine flour and 1 teaspoon each salt and pepper in a shallow dish.
2. Whisk together eggs and 2 tablespoons water in another dish. Combine cornmeal, 1 teaspoon salt, and remaining 1 teaspoon pepper in a third dish.
3. Sprinkle catfish with remaining ¼ teaspoon salt. Dredge fillets, 1 at time, in flour mixture, shaking off excess; dip in egg mixture, and dredge in cornmeal mixture, shaking off excess.
4. Place on a wire rack in a jelly-roll pan.
5. Pour oil to depth of 2 inches in a cast-iron Dutch oven. Heat over medium high heat to 350^0 F.
6. Fry fillets, 2 at a time, in hot oil 6 minutes or until done.
7. Drain on a wire rack over paper towels. Serve with pickled peppers.

Lemon Brown Rice Pilaf:

Serves: 4

Macros per serving:
Calories: 265.3
Protein: 4.4 grams
Fat: 14.3 grams
Carbohydrates: 15 grams

What you'll need:

- 1 tablespoon extra-virgin olive oil
- 1 cup carrots, diced
- 4 cups leeks, light green and white parts only
- 1 teaspoon dried oregano
- 1 cup brown rice
- 2 cups water
- 1 tablespoon chicken stock
- 2 tablespoons lemon juice, freshly squeezed
- 2 tablespoons lemon zest, grated
- Pinch of salt
- Pinch of white pepper

How to make it:

1. Using a large saucepan, heat the olive oil. Cook carrots, leeks, and oregano for 5 minutes, stirring occasionally until tender.
2. Add in brown rice. Cook for 1 minute whilst stirring constantly.
3. Pour water and stock powder. Bring mixture to a boil.
4. Reduce the heat and allow simmering for 15 minutes.
5. Remove from the saucepan and allow standing for 3 minutes.
6. Tip in lemon juice and zest. Season with salt and pepper. Serve.

Delightful and Authentic Shrimp Rolls:

Serves: 12

Macros per serving:
Calories: 84
Protein: 7 grams
Fat: 2 grams
Carbohydrates: 10 grams

What you'll need:

- 6 large shrimp, peeled, halved and boiled
- Red leaf lettuce as needed
- 2 medium sized julienned carrots
- 1 julienned medium seedless cucumber
- 1 sliced avocado
- 1 ounce of cellophane noodles
- 1 tablespoon of seasoned rice vinegar
- Fresh basil
- Fresh bunch of cilantro
- Spring roll wrappers for wrapping

How to make it:

1. Cover cellophane noodles with boiling water and rest for about 10 minutes.
2. Drain the noodles and add the rice wine vinegar. Toss well.
3. Fill a pie plate fill about half way with water.
4. Submerge spring roll wrappers in the water one by one for about 10-30 seconds until they are soft.
5. Lay the softened wrappers on a large piece of parchment paper.
6. Place about 3 shrimp halves, cut side up, in the middle of the bottom half of each wrapper.
7. Arrange the rest of the ingredients alongside the shrimp, making sure to keep an inch clear on either side.
8. Bring the bottom of the wrapper over the whole pile and roll gently.
9. Tuck up the ends as you keep on rolling.
10. Keep repeating until all of the wrappers are rolled nicely.
11. Cut each roll into three pieces and serve with your favorite dipping sauce!

Chicken Curry with Spinach:

Serves: 4

Macros per serving:
Calories: 370
Protein: 57 grams
Fat: 10.6 grams
Carbohydrates: 9 grams

What you'll need:

- 2 chicken breasts, boneless, skinless, chopped into bite sized pieces.
- 1 small onion, halved, sliced
- 1 cup chicken stock
- 1 small red bell pepper, thinly sliced
- 3 bunches fresh spinach, rinsed
- ½ tablespoon fresh ginger, minced
- 2 cloves garlic, sliced
- 1 teaspoon curry powder
- ¼ teaspoon turmeric powder
- 6 tablespoons coconut milk
- White pepper powder to taste
- Salt to taste

How to make it:

1. Boil a pot of water and add spinach to it. Boil for a minute and drain.
2. Press to squeeze out the excess moisture. Sprinkle salt and pepper and set aside.
3. Place a nonstick pan over medium low heat. Add onions and sauté for 5 minutes.
4. Add ginger and garlic and sauté for a couple of minutes until fragrant.
5. Add turmeric and curry powder and sauté for a few seconds.
6. Add stock, chicken, coconut milk and simmer for 5-6 minutes. Add bell pepper and cook until the chicken is tender.
7. To serve: Place blanched spinach on serving plates and place chicken mixture over it.

Lamb Cutlets:

Serves: 9

Macros per serving:
Calories: 318
Protein: 40 grams
Fat: 43 grams
Carbohydrates: 35 grams

What you'll need:

- 800 grams of lamb mince
- 3 slice of bread
- 1/3 cup of milk
- 1 onion
- 1 teaspoon of salt
- Black ground pepper to taste
- 1 small bunch of fresh herbs
- Sunflower oil
- Flour for breading

How to make it:

1. Pieces of bread place the milk until they become soft and absorb the milk.
2. Pieces of bread put in a bowl of milk, until they become soft and absorb the milk.
3. Now you need to grind a large onion. You can use a blender. Also using a blender, you can grind the soaked bread.
4. After that, you should add the onions, bread to the mince, and mix thoroughly. Salt, pepper minced to taste, and add the finely chopped herbs.
5. Mix again. Fry the culets in a small amount of sunflower oil, because the mince is fat and fat will be heated during the frying process.
6. Fry on low heat so that the cutlets do not burn. You can cover them with a lid during the roasting of the second side for few minutes.
7. Cool the cutlets. Put them in a container, and warp it with foil and freeze.
8. When necessary, take the nuggets, and reheat in the microwave and enjoy an excellent dish.

Lemon Garlic Chicken:

Serves: 4

Macros per serving:
Calories: 250
Protein: 24.5 grams
Fat: 6.62 grams
Carbohydrates: 10.93 grams

What you'll need:

- 1 garlic clove, minced
- 2 tablespoons lemon juice, freshly squeezed
- 1 tablespoon extra-virgin olive oil
- 1 teaspoon dried thyme
- ¼ teaspoon salt
- Pinch of ground nutmeg
- Pinch of paprika
- Pinch of ground white pepper
- 4 skinless boneless chicken breasts

How to make it:

1. Preheat the oven to 375^0 F.
2. In a resalable freezer bag, combine olive oil, garlic, lemon juice, salt, nutmeg, thyme, paprika, and white pepper.
3. Shake plastic bag to make sure the ingredients are well combined.
4. Place the chicken breasts inside the resalable bag to marinade. Refrigerate for 1 hour.
5. Transfer marinated chicken breast in a casserole. Bake for 45 minutes. Serve.

Nutty Squash and Eggs:

Serves: 6

Macros per serving:
Calories: 198
Protein: 8 grams
Fat: 12 grams
Carbohydrates: 17 grams

What you'll need:

- 2 acorn squash
- 6 whole eggs
- 2 tablespoons of extra virgin olive oil
- Salt as needed
- Pepper as needed
- 5-6 pitted dates
- 8 walnut halves
- Fresh bunch of parsley for garnish
- Maple syrup if desired

How to make it:

1. Preheat oven to 375⁰ F.
2. Slice squashes crosswise into 3 slices, ¾ inch thick.
3. Remove seeds so that each slice of squash has a hole in the middle.
4. Line a baking sheet with parchment paper and arrange squash slices on the baking sheet.
5. Season with pepper and salt and bake for 20 minutes. Chop walnuts and dates.
6. Remove pan from oven and drizzle a bit of olive oil over the squash slices.
7. Crack an egg directly into the hole in the center of each squash slice and season with pepper and salt.
8. Sprinkle with walnuts and dates and bake for 10 minute more.
9. Garnish with parsley and maple syrup. Serve!

Ginger and Turmeric Grilled Chicken:

Serves: 4

Macros per serving:
Calories: 230
Protein: 48 grams
Fat: 10 grams
Carbohydrates: 3 grams

What you'll need:

- 1 teaspoon lime juice
- ½ teaspoon salt
- ½ teaspoon pepper
- ½ teaspoon cumin
- 1 teaspoon coriander
- 1 teaspoon ginger
- 1 teaspoon turmeric
- 2 garlic
- 1 teaspoon olive oil
- ½ can coconut milk
- 4 chicken breast

How to make it:

1. Begin by mixing together your marinade. Do this by taking a small bowl and mixing together the salt, pepper, lime juice, coriander, ginger, turmeric, garlic, olive oil, and coconut milk.
2. Pour this mixture over the chicken and allow it to marinade for at least one hour. If you have the time, allow this to soak overnight for maximum flavor.
3. When the chicken is ready, place it in a medium pan over medium heat and cook for five or six minutes on either side.
4. For extra flavor, squeeze some fresh lime juice over the chicken.
5. Portion the chicken out and enjoy with your favorite vegetable or rice.

Cauliflower and Lentil Curry:

Serves: 4

Macros per serving:
Calories: 133
Protein: 5 grams
Fat: 5.3 grams
Carbohydrates: 19.4 grams

What you'll need:

- 3 tablespoons vegetable oil
- 1 onion, finely chopped
- 1 fat garlic clove, finely chopped
- 25g fresh root ginger, grated
- 2 teaspoons ground coriander
- 2 teaspoons ground cumin
- ½ teaspoon ground turmeric
- 75g red split lentils
- 150ml vegetable stock, hot
- 1 cauliflower, cut into small florets
- 1 large carrot, peeled and diced
- 400ml can coconut milk
- 75g frozen green beans, thawed
- 3 tablespoons chopped fresh coriander
- 1 tablespoon lemon juice
- Salt and freshly ground black pepper
- Sprig of fresh coriander to garnish

How to make it:

1. Heat 2 tablespoons of the oil in a large saucepan and gently cook the onion for 10 minutes, stirring frequently, until soft and translucent.
2. Add the garlic, ginger, ground coriander, cumin and turmeric and cook for 2 minutes, stirring all the time.
3. Stir in the lentils, and then pour in the stock. Bring to the boil, then reduce the heat, cover and gently simmer for 10 minutes.
4. Meanwhile, heat the remaining 1 tablespoon oil in a frying pan and fry the cauliflower for 2-3 minutes until lightly browned.
5. Add to the lentil mixture with the carrots and coconut milk.
6. Bring the curry back to a gentle simmer and cook for a further 10 minutes or until the vegetables are tender. Stir in the beans and cook for 3-4 minutes.
7. Stir in the chopped coriander and lemon juice, then season to taste with salt and pepper.
8. Spoon onto a warmed serving dish and garnish with a sprig of fresh coriander.

Chicken Vegetable bundles:

Serves: 4

Macros per serving:
Calories: 233.1
Protein: 42.2 grams
Fat: 2.9 grams
Carbohydrates: 8.2 grams

What you'll need:

- 4 skinless chicken breasts, cut lengthwise
- 14 snow peas
- 1 zucchini, cut into ½ inch strips
- 1 sweet potato, cut into ½ inch strips
- 1 tablespoon olive oil
- 2 garlic cloves, finely chopped
- 1 medium onion, halved, thickly sliced
- 1 cup mushrooms, sliced
- 1 teaspoon dried sage
- ¼ teaspoon salt
- Pinch of ground white pepper
- 1 can almond milk, unsweetened
- 3 tablespoons cornstarch
- 2 tablespoons water
- 1 teaspoon lemon juice, freshly squeezed

How to make it:

1. Flatten chicken breast and place one quarter of zucchini strips, snow peas, and sweet potato strips on half of the chicken breast.
2. Fold the remaining half over the veggies.
3. Meanwhile, in a nonstick skillet, heat the olive oil. Sauté onion, garlic, sage, mushrooms, salt, and pepper. Cook for 4 minutes or until tender. Pour almond milk.
4. Add in chicken, seam side down. Bring mixture to a boil.
5. Reduce the heat and allow simmering for 20 minutes.
6. In a bowl, combine water and cornstarch. Pour over the mixture.
7. Continue cooking for 3 more minutes. Add in lemon juice. Serve.

Ancient Fish Roast of the Greeks:

Serves: 2

Macros per serving:
Calories: 388
Protein: 23 grams
Fat: 13 grams
Carbohydrates: 42 grams

What you'll need:

- 5 pounds of small potatoes cut into wedges
- 1/2 sliced onion
- 2 roughly chopped garlic cloves
- ½ teaspoon of dried oregano
- 2 tablespoons of olive oil
- ½ lemon cut into wedges
- 2 large tomatoes cut into wedges
- 2 fresh skinless Pollock fillets
- Just a small handful of roughly chopped parsley

How to make it:

1. Preheat oven to 350^0 F.
2. Place onion, oregano, potatoes, olive oil and garlic in a roasting pan.
3. Season the mixture with salt and pepper and mix everything well.
4. Roast the mix for about 15 minutes, then turn and roast for another 15 minutes.
5. Add fish, tomatoes and lemon to the mix and bake for another 10 minutes.
6. Scatter with parsley and serve.

Kale Chickpea Mash:

Serves: 4

Macros per serving:
Calories: 409
Protein: 15 grams
Fat: 15 grams
Carbohydrates: 53 grams

What you'll need:

- 4 cups cooked chickpeas
- 4 tablespoons garlic, minced
- 2 bunches kale, discard hard ribs and stems, chopped
- 2 shallots, chopped
- 4 tablespoons extra virgin olive oil
- 4 tablespoons liquid amino or soy sauce
- Salt to taste
- 1 teaspoon dried thyme

How to make it:

1. Place a skillet over medium heat. Add oil.
2. When oil is hot, add onion and garlic. Sauté until onions are golden brown.
3. Add kale and sauté until the kale wilts. Add rest of the ingredients and cook for a while.
4. Mash with a fork to the consistency you desire and serve.

Chicken with Broccoli:

Serves: 4

Macros per serving:
Calories: 249
Protein: 27 grams
Fat: 0.7 grams
Carbohydrates: 14.6 grams

What you'll need:

- 2 cups broccoli florets
- 1 lb. chicken breasts, sliced
- 1 inch piece ginger, peeled and chopped
- 1 red bell pepper, seeded and sliced
- 4 teaspoons soy sauce
- 1 tablespoon honey, raw
- 1 tablespoon rice wine vinegar
- 2 scallions, fresh and diced
- 2 cloves garlic, chopped
- 1 carrot, julienned
- Sesame oil as needed
- Vegetable oil as needed
- 2 cups rice, cooked

How to make it:

1. Start by whisking your rice wine vinegar, soy sauce and honey together. Make sure it's mixed well.
2. Heat the vegetable oil over high heat in your wok, and then add half of your garlic, scallion and ginger with your chicken into the pan. Fry for about two minutes. Your chicken should start to brown.
3. Pour in your soy sauce mixture, and then simmer until your chicken glazes. Set it to the side.
4. Place your pan over high heat again, swirling in more of your vegetable oil, adding in the rest of your garlic, scallion and ginger. Add in your bell peppers, carrot and broccoli. Fry for one to two minutes before adding in a third a cup of water.
5. Cover your wok, allowing your vegetables to steam until they are tender but crisp. This should take about five minutes.
6. Uncover your pan, adding in the rest of your soy sauce mixture, and then cook for another one to two minutes.
7. Add your chicken back in, and stir to combine. Drizzle lightly with sesame oil.
8. Divide your rice between your containers, and then top with your stir fry.
9. Allow to cool before freezing.

Grilled Catfish Fillets with Tomato Salad:

Serves: 4

Macros per serving:
Calories: 167.5
Protein: 16.4 grams
Fat: 8.3 grams
Carbohydrates: 5.4 grams

What you'll need:

For the Tomato Salad:

- 2 ripe salad tomatoes, cubed
- 2 large green tomatoes, cubed
- 1 leek, minced
- ¼ pound cherry tomatoes, quartered
- 1 tablespoon balsamic vinegar
- Pinch, generous fresh cilantro, minced
- Pinch of sea salt
- Pinch of black pepper

Fish Fillets:

- 4 catfish fillets
- 2 tablespoons Spanish paprika powder
- ½ teaspoon sea salt
- 1 teaspoon red pepper flakes

How to make it:

1. In a bowl, put together ripe salad tomatoes, green tomatoes, leek, cherry tomatoes, balsamic vinegar, cilantro, salt, and pepper.
2. Toss gently until well-combined. Place salad mix inside the refrigerator until ready to serve.
3. To make the fish, set the grill pan on medium high heat.
4. In a small bowl, combine marinade ingredients- paprika, salt, and red pepper flakes. Dredge fish on the marinade sauce.
5. Grill for 5 minutes on each side. Flip and grill for 3 minutes on the other side.
6. Transfer grilled fish to a platter with aluminum foil. Let rest for 2 minutes.
7. Serve by placing fish fillets on a serving platter with tomato salad on the side. Squeeze lime juice over fillet.

Chicken and Herbal Pillared:

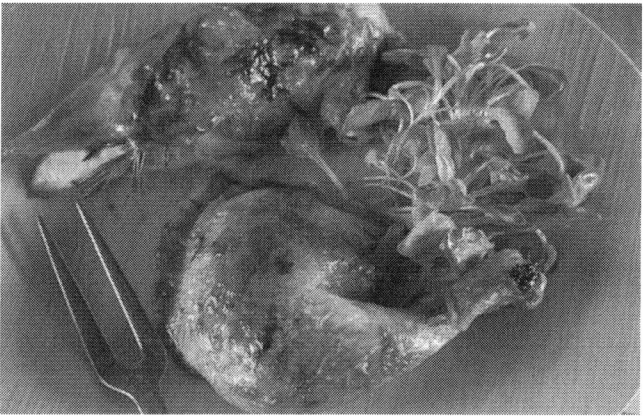

Serves: 6

Macros per serving:
Calories: 240
Protein: 32 grams
Fat: 12 grams
Carbohydrates: 1 gram

What you'll need:

- 6 skinless chicken breasts
- 2 tablespoons of olive oil
- ½ tablespoon of balsamic vinegar
- 140g of rocket
- 25g of parmesan
- Lemon wedges

For Marinade:

- 2 garlic cloves
- ½ teaspoon salt
- Pinch of black pepper
- 3 finely chopped rosemary sprigs
- 6 finely shredded sage leaves
- Zest of 1 lemon and juice of ½ lemon
- 3 tablespoons of olive oil

How to make it:

1. Pound chicken breasts between 2 sheets of baking parchment until they are about ¼ inch thick.
2. Transfer the breast to a baking dish. Mash garlic with salt.
3. Add rosemary and sage. Stir in juice, lemon zest, pepper and olive oil.
4. Pound again and mix well. Pour the mixture over chicken.
5. Cover and refrigerate for 2 hours.
6. Heat grill and spread the coals evenly. Cook the chicken for about 1-2 minutes on each side.
7. Remove from heat and let them rest for a while. In a large bowl, whisk balsamic vinegar and oil.
8. Add rocket and mix. Top with shaved parmesan.
9. Serve this salad with chicken breasts. Enjoy!

Hot Paprika Chicken Breast:

Serves: 6

Macros per serving:
Calories: 248
Protein: 29 grams
Fat: 13 grams
Carbohydrates: 1 gram

What you'll need:

- 6 chicken breasts, skinless, boneless, chop into chunks
- 4 tablespoons olive oil
- 4 tablespoons Spanish smoked paprika
- 3 tablespoons lemon juice
- 1½ tablespoons maple syrup
- 3 teaspoons garlic, minced
- Salt to taste
- Pepper powder to taste

How to make it:

1. Mix together all the ingredients except the chicken to make the sauce.
2. Season the chicken with salt and pepper.
3. Pour 1/3 of the sauce to a casserole dish. Place the chicken pieces on top of it.
4. Pour the remaining sauce all over the chicken pieces.
5. Bake in preheated oven at 350° F for about 30 minutes or until done.

Risotto with Shrimps:

Serves: 5

Macros per serving:
Calories: 359
Protein: 24 grams
Fat: 5 grams
Carbohydrates: 53 grams

What you'll need:

- 1 cup of rice
- 100-150 ml of cream
- 150 grams of shrimp
- 200 grams of white mushrooms
- 3 cloves of garlic

How to make it:

1. Cook the rice for 20 minutes. After this, chop the white mushrooms and fry them for 2 minutes on a low heat.
2. Add the shrimp to the white mushrooms and fry for 2 minutes on a low heat. Fill a little cream.
3. Salt and pepper you should add to taste. After this, simmer the shrimps with vegetables. Then add the garlic to the shrimp.
4. Wait until the cream soaks into the contents. Add the cooked rice and a little cream to the shrimps, and fry for another 2-3 minutes.
5. For freezing, use the bag with zip lock. Put all the ingredients in it. Then pump the air out of the bag. Freeze.
6. When necessary, unfreeze the bag. Content place in the pan and cook for 25 minutes.
7. Next, you can enjoy a delicious dinner.

Asian Chicken Salad:

Serves: 2

Macros per serving:
Calories: 370
Protein: 19 grams
Fat: 6 grams
Carbohydrates: 64 grams

What you'll need:

For salad:

- ½ head purple cabbage, shredded
- ½ head green cabbage, shredded
- 3 cups chicken, cooked, shredded
- 1 can pineapple tidbits, drained
- 1 avocado, cubed
- ¼ cup raw cashew nuts, roasted
- 1 handful cilantro leaves, roughly torn
- 1 carrot, julienned
- ½ red bell pepper, julienned
- 10 stalks chives, minced

For dressing:

- 3 tablespoons boiled water
- 2 tablespoons Stevie
- 2 tablespoons rice wine vinegar
- ¼ teaspoon sesame oil
- ½ cup peanut butter, organic
- 2 teaspoons salt
- 1 lime, freshly juiced

How to make it:

1. For the dressing, combine boiled water, Stevie, rice wine vinegar, sesame oil, peanut butter, salt, and lime juice in an owl.
2. Stir until all ingredients are well combined.
3. For the salad, put together purple and green cabbage, shredded chicken, pineapple tidbits.
4. Avocado, cashew nuts, cilantro leaves, carrots, red bell pepper, and chives.
5. Drizzle in just enough dressing. Toss well to combine. Serve.

Authentic Spanish Gazpacho:

Serves: 4

Macros per serving:
Calories: 120
Protein: 6 grams
Fat: 8 grams
Carbohydrates: 7 grams

What you'll need:

- 100g of baby spinach
- 2 garlic cloves
- 1 large chopped and seeded cucumber
- 1//2 seeded green chili
- ½ small bunch of parsley
- ½ small bunch of basil
- ½ small bunch of mint
- 1 ripe and stoned avocado (peeled)
- 4 topped and tailed spring onions
- 200g of natural yogurt
- 2 tablespoons of sherry vinegar
- Just a drizzle of extra virgin olive oil
- A handful of pea shoots
- Flower petals
- Flower ice cubes (explained in recipe)

How to make it:

1. To make flower ice cubes, fill an ice cube tray with water, add petals such as rose, borage, pansy or viola, and freeze.
2. In a blender, add all ingredients except the pea shoots, ice cubes and oil.
3. Blend on high, adding water as necessary to attain a soupy consistency.
4. Taste the mixture and season with salt, pepper and vinegar if needed.
5. Chill for about 24 hours.
6. Pour the soup into a serving bowl and add flower ice cubes.
7. Scatter with pea shoots and serve!

Coconut Chicken Curry:

Serves: 4

Macros per serving:
Calories: 555
Protein: 8 grams
Fat: 34 grams
Carbohydrates: 55 grams

What you'll need:

- 1½ pounds chicken breast
- 1 cup coconut milk
- 3 tablespoons canola oil
- 1½ cups vegetables broth
- 1½ tablespoons mild curry powder
- 3 tablespoons basil, chopped
- ½ package frozen haricots verts, cook according to instructions on the package
- Salt to taste

How to make it:

1. Mix together 1-tablespoon curry powder and 1-½ tablespoons oil and rub it on to the chicken breast.
2. Place an ovenproof skillet over high heat. Add remaining oil. When oil is heated, add the chicken and cook until brown on all the sides.
3. Remove from heat and place the skillet in a preheated oven.
4. Bake at 350^0 F for about 15 minutes or until a thermometer when inserted in the center of the chicken shows 155^0 F.
5. Remove the dish from the oven and cool. When cool enough to handle, slice the chicken into him slices.
6. Pour a little coconut milk and curry powder to a saucepan and blend until smooth.
7. Add rest of the coconut milk and vegetable broth and place the saucepan over medium heat and simmer until the mixture is slightly thick.
8. Add basil and mix. Remove from heat.
9. To serve: Arrange haricots verts over individual serving plates. Place pork slices over it. Pour sauce over pork and serve.

Chicken with Quinoa and Veggies:

Serves: 2

Macros per serving:
Calories: 453
Protein: 23.8 grams
Fat: 23.8 grams
Carbohydrates: 35.8 grams

What you'll need:

- 1 cup rinsed quinoa
- 2 cups chicken broth
- 2 tablespoons extra-virgin olive oil
- 2 garlic scopes, chopped
- 1 small onion, chopped
- 2 skinless, boneless chicken breast halves cut into strips
- 2 tablespoons extra-virgin olive oil
- 1 zucchini, diced
- 1 tomato, died
- 4 ounces crumbled feta cheese
- 8 fresh basil leaves
- 1 tablespoon lime juice

How to make it:

1. Bring the quinoa and chicken broth to a boil in a saucepan; reduce heat to simmer and cover the pan.
2. Simmer until the broth is absorbed, the quinoa is fluffy, and the white line is visible in the grain, about 12 minutes.
3. Heat 2 tablespoons of olive oil in a skillet; cook and stir the garlic scopes and onion until onion is translucent, about 5 minutes.
4. Stir in the chicken breast strips and cook until the chicken is still slightly pink in the middle, about 5 more minutes.
5. Remove the chicken meat and set aside.
6. Pour 2 more tablespoons of olive oil in the skillet and cook and stir the zucchini and tomato until the zucchini is tender, 5 to 8 minutes.
7. Return chicken to skillet and sprinkle with feta cheese, basil leaves, and lime juice.
8. Cook until the chicken is fully cooked and hot, about 10 more minutes. Serve over hot quinoa.

Quick Fry Chicken with Vegetable Rice:

Serves: 3

Macros per serving:
Calories: 387
Protein: 21.7 grams
Fat: 3 grams
Carbohydrates: 70 grams

What you'll need:

- 3 cups brown rice, cooked
- 2 tablespoons olive oil
- 2 pounds chicken thigh fillets, diced
- 1 can water chestnuts, quartered
- 1 head cauliflower, cut into bite-sized florets
- 1 garlic clove, minced
- 1 thumb-sized ginger, grated
- 1 red bell pepper, julienned
- 2 stalks leeks, minced, reserve some for garnish
- ¾ cups chicken broth, fat-free, low sodium
- Pinch of salt
- Pinch of black pepper
- 1 tablespoon fish sauce
- 4 tablespoons water
- ½ tablespoon cornstarch
- 1 teaspoon Stevie
- Leeks, minced, for garnish

How to make it:

1. Heat the olive oil in a pan. Sauté garlic, ginger, and leeks for 3 minutes or until tender and aromatic.
2. Add in chicken and cook until golden brown in color.
3. Put water chestnuts, cauliflower, garlic clove, ginger, red bell pepper, leeks, and chicken broth. Cover and cook for 15 minutes.
4. Season mixture with salt, pepper, and fish sauce. Dissolve cornstarch in water.
5. Stir in Stevie. Allow mixture to boil for 10 minutes or until the sauce thickens.
6. To serve: place cooked brown rice on a plate.
7. Ladle quick fry chicken and veggies. Garnish with leeks. Serve.

Very Worthy Fish Stew:

Serves: 2

Macros per serving:
Calories: 346
Protein: 42 grams
Fat: 8 grams
Carbohydrates: 20 grams

What you'll need:

- 1 tablespoon of olive oil
- 1 teaspoon of fennel seeds
- 2 diced carrots
- 2 diced celery stalks
- 2 finely chopped garlic cloves
- 2 thinly sliced leeks
- 400g can of chopped tomatoes
- 500 ml of hot fish stock
- 2 skinless Pollock fillets cut into chunks
- 85g of raw shelled king prawns

How to make it:

1. Heat oil in a large pan over medium-high heat.
2. Add carrots, fennel seed and celery.
3. Cook everything for about 5 minutes until the veggies are soft.
4. Add tomatoes, stock and leeks.
5. Season with salt and pepper and bring to a boil.
6. Reduce the heat to low and simmer for about 20 minutes until it becomes a thick sauce.
7. Add fish and prawns. Cook for about 2 minutes.
8. Once done, ladle the soup into serving bowls and serve!

Beef and Broccoli Stir Fry:

Serves: 3

Macros per serving:
Calories: 266
Protein: 32 grams
Fat: 12 grams
Carbohydrates: 6 grams

What you'll need:

- 1 pound beef, top steak, cut into ¼ inch slant slices
- 1 large head broccoli, cut into florets, slice the stalk into thin strips
- 6 cloves garlic, minced
- 2 tablespoons fresh ginger, peeled minced
- 2 red chili peppers, minced
- 2 teaspoons crushed red pepper flakes
- 4 tablespoons canola oil
- 4 tablespoons tamari or coconut amino or soy sauce
- 3 cups beef broth
- 2 tablespoons sesame seeds
- ¼ cup water

How to make it:

1. Mix together in a bowl, beef, soy sauce and garlic and marinate for 15-20 minutes.
2. Mix together in small bowl, broth, vinegar, red pepper flakes and ginger root.
3. Place a large nonstick skillet over medium high heat. Add 2 tablespoons oil.
4. When oil is heated, add only the beef and cook until brown. Remove from the pan and set aside.
5. Place the pan back on heat. Add remaining oil when oil is heated; add broccoli and chili pepper and sauté for a minute.
6. Add water, cover and cook until broccoli is tender. Stir frequently.
7. Add broth mixture and cooked beef. Simmer for 3-4 minutes.
8. Remove from heat. Sprinkle sesame seeds and serve.

Crusted Herb Pork Chops:

Serves: 4

Macros per serving:
Calories: 298
Protein: 25 grams
Fat: 10 grams
Carbohydrates: 5 grams

What you'll need:

- 1 teaspoon olive oil
- ½ teaspoon pepper
- ½ teaspoon salt
- 1 teaspoon parsley
- 1 teaspoon thyme
- ½ cup panko breadcrumbs
- 2 teaspoons Dijon mustard
- 4 pork chops

How to make it:

1. Begin by heating your oven to 450° F.
2. Next, you will prep your pork chops by rubbing them with the Dijon mustard.
3. In small bowl, combine the salt, pepper, and parsley, thyme, and panko breadcrumbs. For a healthier version, try to get whole wheat breadcrumbs.
4. When you are ready, dip the mustard covered pork chops into the breadcrumbs. Be sure that they are coated.
5. Once they are ready, go ahead and heat a large skillet over medium heat and put your olive oil in. Sauté the chop for two or three minutes on each side before popping it into the oven.
6. Keep the pork chops in the oven for eight to ten minutes before removing and allowing cooling. Portion into your containers and serve with your favorite side.

Oatmeal-Crusted Chicken Wings and Veggies:

Serves: 4

Macros per serving:
Calories: 288
Protein: 23.3 grams
Fat: 1.2 grams
Carbohydrates: 24.1 grams

What you'll need:

- 4 large chicken wings
- 6 green beans, sliced into long slivers
- 1 sweet potato, sliced into long slivers
- 1 small aborigine, sliced into long slivers
- 1 carrot, sliced into long slivers
- 1 teaspoon salt
- 1 teaspoon ground black pepper
- 1 teaspoon Spanish paprika
- 1 cup almond flour, finely milled
- 2 eggs, lightly beaten
- 1 cup steel-cut oats
- Olive oil cooking oil, enough to fill fryer

How to make it:

1. Season chicken wings, green beans, sweet potato, aborigine, and carrots with salt, pepper, and paprika. Let it sit for 15-30 minutes.
2. Meanwhile, in separate bowls, pour almond flour, eggs, and then oats.
3. Heat the oil in a pan. Fry chicken wings and vegetables for 3 minutes or until golden brown.
4. Drain in paper towels. Serve.

Upbeat Spicy Pumpkin Chili:

Serves: 5

Macros per serving:
Calories: 312
Protein: 27.4 grams
Fat: 16.2 grams
Carbohydrates: 13.5 grams

What you'll need:

- 2 tablespoons coconut oil
- 3 cups of chopped yellow onion
- 8 cloves of chopped garlic
- 1 pound of ground turkey
- 2 15-ounce cans of fire roasted tomatoes
- 2 cups of pumpkin puree
- 1 cup of chicken broth
- 2 tablespoons of honey
- 4 teaspoons of chili spice
- 1 teaspoon of ground cinnamon
- 1 teaspoon of sea salt

How to make it:

1. In a large pot, heat coconut oil over medium heat.
2. Add garlic and onion and sauté for 5 minutes.
3. Add ground turkey and break it up with a spatula
4. Cook for 5 minutes.
5. Add the remaining ingredients and simmer for 15 minutes uncovered.
6. Add chicken broth, heat, and serve with salad!

Chicken Taco Pizza:

Serves: 8

Macros per serving:
Calories: 580
Protein: 38 grams
Fat: 29 grams
Carbohydrates: 43 grams

What you'll need:

- 2 whole wheat pizza crusts, freshly made or frozen
- 2 frozen chicken breasts, skinless, boneless, thawed, chopped into bite sized pieces
- 2 cups frozen corn, thawed
- 2 cups cooked black beans, rinsed, drained
- 1 cup salsa + extra to serve
- 2 cups part skim mozzarella cheese, grated, divided
- ½ cup fresh cilantro, chopped

How to make it:

1. Lay the pizza crusts a large baking sheet. Divide salsa and spread over both the crusts.
2. Sprinkle half the cheese over the salsa.
3. Sprinkle beans, corn, and chicken over the cheese. Finally top with the remaining cheese.
4. Bake in a preheated oven 425^0 F. until the cheese is melted and slightly brown.
5. Remove from the oven and sprinkle cilantro on it.
6. Cut into wedges and serve with some salsa.

Easy Turkey Chili:

Serves: 8

Macros per serving:
Calories: 378
Protein: 35 grams
Fat: 4 grams
Carbohydrates: 26 grams

What you'll need:

- .10 teaspoon cayenne pepper
- 2 teaspoons oregano
- 3 teaspoons chili powder
- 1 packet Stevie
- ½ teaspoon pepper
- ½ teaspoon salt
- 2 jalapenos
- 2 bell peppers
- 1 can kidney beans
- ½ teaspoon hot sauce
- 3 teaspoon tomato paste
- 1 can diced tomatoes
- 1 can crushed tomatoes
- 1 teaspoon olive oil
- 5 garlic
- 1 onion
- 2 lbs. ground turkey

How to make it:

1. To start, you will want to place your olive oil, onion, and garlic into a large pot and allow this to cook for a couple of minutes.
2. Once you can smell the garlic, add in your turkey and cook it for ten minutes or until it is brown.
3. Finally, toss in the rest of the ingredients from the list above. Be sure to stir everything together so it becomes well combined.
4. Allow this to cook for an hour over a low heat and then portion into your containers.

Almond and Chicken Stir-Fry:

Serves: 2-3

Macros per serving:
Calories: 440
Protein: 30.3 grams
Fat: 8.2 grams
Carbohydrates: 63.2 grams

What you'll need:

- 3 tablespoons olive oil
- Chicken breast fillet, julienned
- 1 white onion, julienned
- 1 cup button mushrooms
- ½ cup pound bok Choy
- ¾ cup chicken stock
- Tablespoons light soy sauce
- ¼ cup water
- ¼ teaspoon black pepper
- ¼ teaspoon sea salt
- ½ cup garlic roasted almonds, chopped

Cornstarch:

- Tablespoon cornstarch
- 1 tablespoon water

How to make it:

1. In a bowl, dissolve cornstarch in water. Set aside.
2. Meanwhile, pour olive oil. Cook chicken for 3 minutes or until the lightly seared.
3. Stir in onions, button mushrooms, bok Choy, chicken stock, soy sauce, and water.
4. Season with salt and pepper. Stir fry for 5 minutes.
5. Pour cornstarch and continue stirring until the sauce thickens.
6. Spoon an equal amount on plates. Garnish with almonds. Serve.

Goat Cheese Herbal Pancake:

Serves: 2

Macros per serving:
Calories: 254
Protein: 16 grams
Fat: 17 grams
Carbohydrates: 9 grams

What you'll need:

- 1 teaspoon of rapeseed oil, divided
- 2 finely chopped spring onions
- 1 large coarsely grated courgette
- 2 large whole eggs
- 2 tablespoons of chopped basil
- 2 tablespoons water
- 2 teaspoons of thyme leaves
- 50g of soft goat cheese
- 2 chopped medium tomatoes
- 6 calamite olives, rinsed and halved
- 2 handfuls of baby kale
- Radishes as desired

How to make it:

1. Heat ½ teaspoon oil in a skillet or frying pan over medium heat.
2. Add the courgette and spring onions and cook them until they are tender.
3. Transfer cooked vegetables into a bowl. Wash the pan.
4. In another bowl. Beat one egg with 1 tablespoon of water and half of the herbs and black pepper.
5. Heat remaining ½ teaspoon oil in the pan and add the egg mixture, making sure to keep swirling it as it pours.
6. Cook for about 2-3 minutes.
7. Transfer to a serving plate and repeat the process with the remaining egg, herbs, and 1 tablespoon of water.
8. Spread the goat cheese and cooked vegetables over the center of each egg pancake.
9. Roll up the pancake and arrange baby kale, olives, tomatoes and radishes around it on the plate. Serve.

Beef Taco Stuffed Avocadoes:

Serves: 5

Macros per serving:
Calories: 488
Protein: 13 grams
Fat: 42 grams
Carbohydrates: 19 grams

What you'll need:

- ½ pound ground beef
- ¼ cup onions, finely chopped
- ¼ cup bell pepper, finely chopped
- 2 green onions, thinly sliced
- 1 tablespoon olive oil
- ¼ cup sharp cheddar cheese, grated
- 5 small avocadoes, halved, pitted
- 2 teaspoons taco seasoning or more to taste
- Salt to taste

How to make it:

1. Place a skillet over medium heat. Add oil. When the oil is heated, add onion and bell pepper and sauté until onions are translucent.
2. Add beef and sauté until beef is nearly cooked. Add taco seasoning and salt and cook for 2-3 minutes.
3. Remove from heat and add cheese. Mix well.
4. Divide and fill the avocadoes with this mixture. Sprinkle green onions on top.
5. Serve immediately.

Garlicky Lebanese Chicken Thighs:

Serves: 2

Macros per serving:
Calories: 544
Protein: 30 grams
Fat: 40 grams
Carbohydrates: 11 grams

What you'll need:

- Garlic olive oil
- 2 tablespoons ghee
- 4 chicken thighs
- 1 Vidalia onion cut into quarters
- A handful of baby carrots
- 2 roma tomatoes cut in half
- 15 whole cloves of garlic
- Oregano
- Juice of one fresh lemon (sift the seeds out)
- Salt and pepper

How to make it:

1. Heat the oven to 500° F. Glaze the bottom of a cast-iron pan with about 2 teaspoon of garlic olive oil.
2. Add the 4 chicken thighs together, but try to give them space.
3. In between the thighs, wedge in your onions, carrots, garlic gloves and tomatoes.
4. Add at least 1-2 garlic cloves on top of the thighs.
5. Juice the lemon over the thighs. Drizzle more garlic oil over the top of the thighs (about 2 tablespoon). Drizzle the ghee over the thighs.
6. Generously sprinkle oregano over the dish plus salt and pepper to taste. Stick in the oven for 30 minutes.
7. Reduce heat to 350° F. and cook for 20 minutes until cooked to 165° F.
8. Increase oven to Broil (to crisp up the skins) and cook for 5 minutes or until crispy. Remove and enjoy!

Classic Short Ribs with Olives:

Serves: 4

Macros per serving:
Calories: 112.5
Protein: 4.8 grams
Fat: 9.3 grams
Carbohydrates: 1.8 grams

What you'll need:

- Tablespoon dried thyme
- 1 tablespoon fennel seeds
- Tablespoons extra virgin olive oil
- 1 tablespoon black pepper corns
- ½ lbs. beef short ribs
- 2 onions, finely chopped
- 2 cloves garlic, minced
- 2 carrots, finely chopped
- 2 anchovy fillets, finely chopped
- 1 teaspoon sea salt
- ½ teaspoon black pepper corns
- 1 tablespoon vinegar
- 1 can diced tomatoes with juice
- 1 bouquet garn
- 1 cup pitted black olives, chopped

How to make it:

1. Combine thyme, fennel, olive oil, and pepper corns in small bowl. Dredge short ribs and marinade for 2 hours or until ready to use.
2. Meanwhile, in a pan, heat the olive oil. Sauté onion, garlic, carrots, and anchovies. Season with salt and pepper. Set aside. Add in vinegar, tomatoes, and garn.
3. Pour marinated short ribs. Allow the mixture too cook for 15 minutes.
4. Stir in black olives. Cook for another 5 minutes. Serve.

A very Grim and Brooding Blackened Chicken:

Serves: 2

Macros per serving:
Calories: 135
Protein: 24 grams
Fat: 3 grams
Carbohydrates: 0.9 grams

What you'll need:

- ½ teaspoon of paprika
- $1/8$ teaspoon of salt
- ¼ teaspoon of cayenne pepper
- ¼ teaspoon of ground cumin
- ¼ teaspoon of dried thyme
- $1/8$ teaspoon of ground white pepper
- $1/8$ teaspoon of onion powder
- 2 skinless and boneless chicken breasts

How to make it:

1. Preheat oven to 350^0 F.
2. Place a cast iron skillet over high heat for 5 minutes, until smoking hot.
3. In a small bowl, mix salt, paprika, cumin, cayenne, white pepper, thyme and onion powder.
4. Oil chicken breasts with cooking spray, coating evenly on both sides.
5. Coat chicken with the prepared spice mixture.
6. Place the chicken in hot pan and cook for about 1 minute.
7. Turn it over and cook for another 1 minute.
8. Place the cooked chicken on a lightly-greased baking sheet and bake for about 5 minutes until it is no longer pink. Serve!

Lamb Roast with Veggies:

Serves: 2

Macros per serving:
Calories: 240
Protein: 23 grams
Fat: 34 grams
Carbohydrates: 1.3 grams

What you'll need:

- ½ pound lamb stew meat, cut into large cubes
- 2 medium tomatoes
- 1 onion, roughly chopped
- 2 cloves garlic, pressed
- 1 cup button mushrooms, halved
- 2 carrots, peeled, chopped
- 1 tablespoon fresh thyme, finely chopped
- 1 tablespoon fresh rosemary, finely chopped
- 1 cup chicken or lamb stock
- Freshly ground black pepper to taste

How to make it:

1. Blanch the tomatoes in billing water until the skin just starts to crack.
2. Strain the tomatoes and place in cold water and peel the skin. Chop the tomatoes into chunks.
3. Add tomatoes to a large baking dish. Add mushrooms, carrots, onions, lamb, salt, pepper, rosemary, thyme and garlic. Mix well.
4. Place the baking dish in a preheated oven at 325^0 F. and bake for about 2 hours or until the lamb is cooked.
5. Stir a couple of times in between.
6. Serve hot.

Beef Wrapped in Beef Fillet:

Serves: 4

Macros per serving:
Calories: 182
Protein: 23 grams
Fat: 9 grams
Carbohydrates: 2 grams

What you'll need:

- 3 tablespoons olive oil
- Onion, chopped
- 1 garlic, minced
- Cups ground beef
- 1 teaspoon parsley, minced
- ¼ teaspoon dried marjoram
- 1 teaspoon salt
- $1/8$ teaspoon pepper
- Hardboiled eggs, mashed
- Beef fillet, thinly sliced

How to make it:

1. Heat the oil in a pan. Sauté garlic and onion for 3 minutes or until translucent and aromatic.
2. Add in ground beef, parsley, and marjoram. Season with salt and pepper. Stir mixture well.
3. Cook for 5 minutes. Add in egg. Mix well. Place mixture on each beef fillet. Roll up fillet and tie up using a kitchen string or a toothpick.
4. Heat the oil in a pan. Cook beef fillets for 4 minutes or until both sides are cooked through. Serve.

Supremely Secret Wrap of Turkey and Bacon:

Serves: 2

Macros per serving:
Calories: 150
Protein: 6.1 grams
Fat: 13.5 grams
Carbohydrates: 17.5 grams

What you'll need:

For the Pico De Gallo:

- 1 head of iceberg lettuce
- 4 slices of deli turkey
- 4 slices of cooked bacon
- 1 thinly sliced avocado
- 1 thinly sliced Roma tomato

For the Basil Mayo:

- ½ cup of mayonnaise
- 6 large torn basil leaves
- 1 teaspoon lemon juice
- 1 chopped garlic clove
- Salt as needed
- Pepper as needed

How to make it:

1. In a food processor, to combine all basil mayo ingredients and process them until very smooth.
2. Take lettuce leaves and layer with 1 slice of turkey and a generous amount of the previously prepared Basil Mayo.
3. Add a second slice of turkey and follow it with two slices of bacon and a few slices of tomato and avocado.
4. Season with pepper and salt, and fold them as for a burrito.
5. Slice in half and serve chilled.

Chicken parmesan:

Serves: 2

Macros per serving:
Calories: 251
Protein: 31.5 grams
Fat: 9.5 grams
Carbohydrates: 14 grams

What you'll need:

- 2 chicken breasts, skinless, trimmed
- 2 tablespoons arrowroot flour
- ½ cup almond flour
- 2 eggs, beaten
- ¼ teaspoon onion powder
- ½ teaspoon oregano
- ¼ teaspoon garlic powder
- ½ teaspoon basil
- Salt to taste
- Pepper to taste
- Crushed red pepper flakes to taste

How to make it:

1. Add flours, spices herbs and salt into a bowl. Mix well.
2. First dip a chicken breast into the egg. Shake off excess egg. Next dredge the chicken into the flour mixture.
3. Dip again into the egg and dredge in the flour. Place on a lined baking sheet.
4. Repeat the above step with the other chicken breast.
5. Bake in a preheated oven at 375^0 F for about 40 minutes.
6. Top with spaghetti sauce and brown rice noodles or zucchini noodles and serve.

Chicken Mango and Cherry Tomato Salad:

Serves: 4

Macros per serving:
Calories: 240
Protein: 10 grams
Fat: 1 gram
Carbohydrates: 7 grams

What you'll need:

- 4 chicken breast fillets
- Onion, chopped
- Garlic cloves, crushed
- 1 root ginger, crushed
- Tablespoons dry white wine
- 1 red bell pepper, chopped
- 1 celery stalk, sliced thinly
- 2 tablespoons honey
- 2 tablespoons soy sauce, sodium reduced
- Pinch of salt
- Pinch of pepper
- 1 mango, cubed
- Cherry tomatoes, halved
- Parsley, chopped, to garnish

How to make it:

1. Preheat the oven to 350⁰ F. Lightly grease a baking sheet.
2. Layer chicken breasts.
3. Meanwhile, using a small saucepan, sauté onion, garlic, ginger, dry white wine, red bell pepper, celery, honey, and sauce. Bring mixture to a brief boil. Pour mixture over the chicken.
4. Bake chicken for 30 minutes.
5. Slide baked chicken to a platter and pour over juices.
6. Serve by placing chicken breasts at the center surrounded by cubed mangoes and cherry tomatoes. Sprinkle parsley.

CONCLUSION:

Thank you for reading this book and having the patience to try the recipes.

I do hope that you gain as much enjoyment reading and experimenting with the meals as I have had writing these books.

If you would like to leave a comment, you can do it at the Order section->Digital order send and also buy paperback, in your Amazon account.

Stay safe and healthy!

Other Books by Tanaya Hill

Keto Diet for Beginners: Amazing and Simple Recipes in One Ketogenic Cookbook, Low-Carb, High-Fat and Weight Loss Recipes.

ASIN: B07F6JZK9M
ISBN-10: 9781983361234

https://www.amazon.com/dp/B07F6JZK9M

The vegetarian keto diet: Delicious and Fitness Vegetarian Keto Recipes For a Healthy Lifestyle and Weight Loss.

ASIN: B07H1BLGLB
ISBN-10: 9781720049654

htttps://www.amazon.com/dp/B07H1BLGLB

Air Fryer Cookbook: The Complete Air Fryer Cookbook-Easy and Delicious Recipes Healthy Meals for Your Family (Simple and Clear Instructions)

ASIN: B07HG1YT85
ISBN-10: 1723796611

https://www.amazon.com/dp/B07HG1YT85

The Instant Pot Cookbook: The Best Easy, Delicious and Healthy Recipes for Your Whole Family and Friends to Cook in Your Electric Instant Pot

ASIN: B07JMPP2M8
ISBN-10: 1729117139

htttps://www.amazon.com/dp/B07JMPP2M8

Made in the USA
San Bernardino, CA
27 April 2019